Dear Parents and Educators,

Welcome to Penguin Young Readers! As parents and educators, you know that each child develops at his or her own pace—in terms of speech, critical thinking, and, of course, reading. Penguin Young Readers recognizes this fact. As a result, each Penguin Young Readers book is assigned a traditional easy-to-read level (1–4) as well as a Guided Reading Level (A–P). Both of these systems will help you choose the right book for your child. Please refer to the back of each book for specific leveling information. Penguin Young Readers features esteemed authors and illustrators, stories about favorite characters, fascinating nonfiction, and more!

Best Friends: The True Story of Owen and Mzee

LEVEL **2**

GUIDED READING LEVEL **I**

This book is perfect for a **Progressing Reader** who:
• can figure out unknown words by using picture and context clues;
• can recognize beginning, middle, and ending sounds;
• can make and confirm predictions about what will happen in the text; and
• can distinguish between fiction and nonfiction.

Here are some **activities** you can do during and after reading this book:
• Nonfiction: Nonfiction books deal with facts and events that are real. Talk about the elements of nonfiction. On a separate sheet of paper, write down the facts you learned about hippos and tortoises from this book.
• Make Connections: In this story, Owen and Mzee become friends even though they are different from each other. Think about one friend who is different from you. How do those differences make your friendship special?

Remember, sharing the love of reading with a child is the best gift you can give!

—Bonnie Bader, EdM
    Penguin Young Readers program

*Penguin Young Readers are leveled by independent reviewers applying the standards developed by Irene Fountas and Gay Su Pinnell in *Matching Books to Readers: Using Leveled Books in Guided Reading*, Heinemann, 1999.

To my great sand sculpture crew and
especially Evan and Jennifer—CS

The illustrator (right) at a sand sculpture contest

Penguin Young Readers
Published by the Penguin Group
Penguin Group (USA) Inc., 375 Hudson Street, New York, New York 10014, USA
Penguin Group (Canada), 90 Eglinton Avenue East, Suite 700, Toronto, Ontario M4P 2Y3, Canada
(a division of Pearson Penguin Canada Inc.)
Penguin Books Ltd, 80 Strand, London WC2R 0RL, England
Penguin Ireland, 25 St Stephen's Green, Dublin 2, Ireland (a division of Penguin Books Ltd)
Penguin Group (Australia), 707 Collins Street, Melbourne, Victoria 3008, Australia
(a division of Pearson Australia Group Pty Ltd)
Penguin Books India Pvt Ltd, 11 Community Centre, Panchsheel Park, New Delhi—110 017, India
Penguin Group (NZ), 67 Apollo Drive, Rosedale, Auckland 0632, New Zealand
(a division of Pearson New Zealand Ltd)
Penguin Books, Rosebank Office Park, 181 Jan Smuts Avenue, Parktown North 2193, South Africa
Penguin China, B7 Jaiming Center, 27 East Third Ring Road North, Chaoyang District, Beijing 100020, China

Penguin Books Ltd, Registered Offices: 80 Strand, London WC2R 0RL, England

Text copyright © 2007 by Penguin Group (USA) Inc. Illustrations copyright © 2007 by Carol Schwartz.
All rights reserved. First published in 2007 by Grosset & Dunlap, an imprint of
Penguin Group (USA) Inc. Published in 2013 by Penguin Young Readers, an imprint of Penguin Group (USA) Inc.,
345 Hudson Street, New York, New York 10014. Manufactured in China.

Library of Congress Control Number: 2006031177

ISBN 978-0-448-44567-0   10 9 8 7 6 5 4 3 2 1

ALWAYS LEARNING   PEARSON

Best Friends

The True Story of Owen and Mzee

by Roberta Edwards
illustrated by Carol Schwartz

Penguin Young Readers
An Imprint of Penguin Group (USA) Inc.

This is a very old giant tortoise.

His name is Mzee

(say: ma-ZEE).

This is a baby hippo named Owen.

Mzee and Owen are best friends.

What do they have in common?

Not much.

Tortoises are reptiles.

So are crocodiles,

snakes, and lizards.

Hippos are mammals.

So are cows and dogs

and people, too!

Like all mammals,

mother hippos give birth

to live babies.

Owen was more than

50 pounds at birth.

He was about

three feet long.

That's a big baby!

Hippos are one

of the biggest

land animals on earth.

Only elephants and rhinos

are bigger.

Owen's mother took
good care of him.
She fed him her milk.
She watched him play
with other little hippos.

He liked to roll in mud.

It kept him cool.

And it got rid of bugs.

Africa

Owen and his mother lived

with a group of hippos.

They lived near a river

on the east coast of Africa.

(The dark dot on the map

shows where.)

She and the older hippos

kept Owen and the other babies

safe from enemies.

Who are hippos' enemies?

Lions and hyenas

and crocodiles.

One day heavy rains came.

It rained and rained.

The river flooded.

The hippos were swept out to sea.

At last the storm ended.

Only one hippo was left.

Owen.

He was just one year old.

And he was all alone.

Still, he was lucky.

Some people saved Owen.

He was hard to catch.

But they got

the little hippo to land.

They named him Owen

after the man who caught him.

Owen needed a new home.

He could not care for himself.

But a new group of hippos

would just turn him away.

The best place was a special zoo.

Owen was driven there.

Haller Park became

Owen's new home.

Do you know who else

lived at Haller Park?

Mzee.

Mzee was the oldest animal there.

He was 130 years old!

His name means

"wise old man."

Mzee lived by a pond.

He was not friends

with other animals.

Not the monkeys

or the bushbucks.

(Bushbucks look like small deer.)

But right away

Owen picked out Mzee.

He ran over to him.

Owen hid behind the old tortoise.

Poor Owen!

He was scared.

Maybe Mzee looked like a hippo

to him.

Mzee hissed at Owen.

Mzee tried to get away.

But no matter where Mzee went,

Owen followed.

The next morning

Owen was curled up at

Mzee's side.

Mzee did not seem to mind.

Little by little

Owen and Mzee became friends.

Now they are best friends.

They take swims together.

They eat their food together.

They sleep side by side.

Owen has no mother.

He has Mzee.

Mzee has Owen.

That is enough for both of them.